Pat –
God bless you
and a belated Happy Birthday
Love, Bill & Joella 1996

Smile!
God loves you
& We do too!

and other

INTO
THE
WOODS
favorite verses

Compiled by
Daughters of St. Paul

ST. PAUL EDITIONS

Nihil Obstat:
   Msgr. John G. Hogan

Imprimatur:
   ✠ Humberto Cardinal Medeiros
   Archbishop of Boston

Unless authorship is indicated
the selections in this volume are,
to the best of our knowledge,
by unknown authors.

Photo Credits:

Gordon Alves—pages 10-11, 19, 22-23, 24, 25, 28-29, 30-31, 66-67, 70-71, 72-73, 74-75, 78-79

Gilbert Lehmbeck—page 26

Paul Prough—pages 20-21, 76-77

Daughters of St. Paul—pages 68-69

Library of Congress Catalog Card Number 73—89937

Printed in U.S.A. by the Daughters of St. Paul
50 St. Paul's Ave., Boston, Ma. 02130

The Daughters of St. Paul are an international
religious congregation serving the Church with
the communications media.

Dedication

To all the people we Daughters of St. Paul
have met on our apostolic visits in offices, factories
stores and homes—the good people who have been
cheered and inspired by the poems and prayers now
collected in this book.

These are the verses often found tacked
on fire station walls, slid under glass-top desks,
taped onto lamp shades, folded neatly in business
men's wallets, hidden in combat helmets,
and thumbtacked onto cork bulletinboards. They
have been mimeographed, xeroxed, carboned, recorded,
and framed by the hundreds.

We hope that this collection will bring just as
much joy, encouragement and peace to many good
people as the individual thoughts already have.

CONTENTS

Into the Woods 10

The Man in the Glass 12

I Asked 14

No Harm Done.. 16

Promise Yourself... 17

Don't Quit.. 18

The Great Transformation 20

Keep Your Courage One More Day 23

Look Up.. 24

For a Sense of Humor 27

Hour by Hour 28

Life's Clock 31

God Bless You.. 32

That You May "B" Happy 33

What Is Christ to Me? 34

Human Relations 35

For Those Growing Old 36

It Shows in Your Face 38

When My Temper Flies 40

Others 45

Teach Me 46

Sowing 47

If 48

Working Girl's Prayer 49

The Teen Commandments 50
Still in Vogue... 51
For Those Who Live Alone 52
The Difference 54
When You Are Tired, Discouraged and Blue 55
"3" 56
There's a Reason 57
My Path.. 58
I Know Something Good About You 60
In Praise of Virtue... 61
Our People 62
Advice 64
Judge Not... 65
Believing 67
Stairs of Opportunity 68
How To Count.. 70
I'll Go Where You Want Me To Go 72
Your Cross 75
Be At Peace.. 76
Even If... 78
Mother's Heart 80
Power of Prayer 81
Christ of Calvary.. 82
Beatitudes for Friends of the Aged 84
Chosen One 86
Take Time... 88
Life 91

into the woods

When
   life's horizon
   is charcoal gray,
   I find my way
   into the woods
   where I can exchange
   my shopworn
   worldly goods
   for new dreams
   and values
   that have been
   waiting there
   for me to choose,
   somewhere
   in the shadows
   of the leaves
   and trees.

One
   sees things
   more clearly then,
   and nearly
   understands it all:

the call
of the wild,
the mild
and tender
whisper of love,
the fallibility
of man,
the commonplace
and odd,
and even...perhaps,
the infallibility
of God.

—Robert Baram

the man in the glass

When you get what you want in your struggle for self
And the world makes you king for a day,
Just go to a mirror and look at yourself,
And see what <u>that</u> man has to say.

For it isn't your father or mother or wife,
Who judgment upon you must pass;
The fellow whose verdict counts most in your life
Is the one staring back from the glass.

He's the fellow to please, never mind all the rest.
For he's with you clear up to the end,
And you've passed your most dangerous, difficult test
If the man in the glass is your friend.

You may fool the whole world down the pathway of
       years
And get pats on the back as you pass,
But your final reward will be heartaches and tears
If you've cheated the man in the glass.

13

I asked

I asked for strength...that I might achieve...
   I was made weak...that I might learn humbly
      to obey.
I asked for health...that I might do greater things...
   I was given infirmity...that I might do better
      things.
I asked for riches...that I might be happy...
   I was given poverty...that I might be wise.
I asked for power...that I might have the praise of
      men...
   I was given weakness...that I might feel the
      need of God.

I asked for all things...that I might enjoy life...
    I was given life...that I might enjoy all things.
I got nothing that I asked for...but everything that
    I had hoped for.
Almost despite myself...my unspoken prayers were
        answered
    ...I am among all men most richly blessed.

no harm done

By swallowing
   evil words
     unsaid

       no one
     has ever yet
     harmed
    his stomach.

—Winston Churchill

promise
yourself...

To be so strong that nothing can disturb your
    peace of mind.
To talk health, happiness and prosperity to every
    person you meet.
To look at the sunny side of everything and make
    your optimism come true.
To think only the best, to work only for the best,
    and expect only the best.
To be just as enthusiastic about the success of
    others as you are about your own.
To forget about the mistakes of the past and to
    press on to greater achievements of the future.
To wear a cheerful countenance at all times and
    give every person you meet a smile.
To give so much time to the improvement of yourself
    that you have no time to criticize others.
To be too big to worry and too noble for anger.
To be too strong for fear and too happy to
    permit the presence of trouble.

—Msgr. Charles McCarthy

17

don't quit

When things go wrong, as they sometimes will,
When the road you're trudging seems all uphill,
When the funds are low and the debts are high,
    And you want to smile,
    But you have to sigh,
When care is pressing you down a bit—
Rest if you must, but don't you quit.

    Life is queer with its twists and turns,
    As every one of us sometimes learns,
    And many a fellow turns about
When he might have won had he stuck it out.
Don't give up though the pace seems slow—
You may succeed with another blow.

    Often the goal is nearer than
    It seems to a faint and faltering man;
    Often the struggler has given up
When he might have captured the victor's cup;
      And he learned too late when the night
      came down,
How close he was to the golden crown.

Success is failure turned inside out—
The silver tint of the clouds of doubt,
And you never can tell how close you are,

It may be near when it seems afar;
So stick to the fight when you're hardest hit,—
It's when things seem worst that you mustn't quit.

the great transformation

Prayer has great power.
It makes a sour heart sweet,
    A sad heart joyful,
    A poor heart rich,
    A foolish heart wise,
    A faint heart bold,
    A sick heart well,
    A blind heart able to see
And a cold heart full of fire!

—St. Mechtild of Mageburg

Our Father, who art in heaven, hallowed be Thy name; Thy kingdom come; Thy will be done on earth as it is in heaven. Give us this day our daily bread; and forgive us our trespasses as we forgive those who trespass against us; and lead us not into temptation, but deliver us from evil. Amen.

keep your courage
one more day

When the day is dark and gloomy
And the fog obscures your view,
And you feel there is no challenge
Waiting anywhere for you;
When it's routine you must follow
Through a dreary weather chart,
And you feel the hand of duty
Like a millstone on your heart;

Face the skies however darkened,
When you ache to turn away
Do the job that lies before you,
Keep your courage one more day.
You can never guess how often
You affect another's life
By the fact you are a doer
Not a quitter in the strife.

look up

When I am tempted to evil
I look to the left and the right
And backward glance, then forward
Contented that no one's in sight.

How much worry and grief I'd avoided;
How often I'd kept out of sin;
If only I looked up towards heaven
And felt God's great power within.

So many times when tormented,
I've looked all around me, in vain
For help, a kind word, understanding,
And received from mankind only pain.

Dear God, from now on, please help me
To turn my eyes quickly above
And see there waiting to help me
The Fount of good and all love.

A God who is "Friend to the Friendless,"
Who is ever "The Someone Who Cares,"
Who is never too busy to listen,
And answer the call of our prayers.

Help me daily to live in Your presence,
Knowing no place is hid from Your view,
That always Your hands reach earthward
If only I'll look up to You.

So many, in sickness, find solace
When flat on their back day by day
Looking up seems to make it so easy
For them to find reason to pray.

For help and strength in my problems
For sympathy, friendship and love
I shall seek it, and share it with others
When I look up and find God above.

— Fr. Joseph P. McCall

for a sense of humor

It was pretty funny
Lord
I have to admit.
But does the laughter
always have to be at my expense?
I'm not the only one
who uses the wrong word
or gets caught in an absurd situation.
I turn out to be the butt
of everyone else's joke
—more so lately.
Or does it only seem that way?
Am I getting too touchy,
too quick to defend myself
against anything that would make me—
well, like the rest of humanity, I guess.
Next time, help me to see
the humor in the situation
and not imagine that people's merriment
is prompted by unkindness.
After all, I am a bit foolish at times
and I suppose I had it coming.
Amen.

—Christopher News Notes

hour by hour

God broke our years to hours and days,
That hour by hour and day by day,
We might be able all along
To keep quite strong.
Should all the weight of life
Be laid across our shoulders,
And the future, rife with woe and struggle,
Meet us face to face at just one place,
We could not go:
Our feet would stop, and so
God lays a little on us every day.
And never, I believe, on all the way
Will burdens bear so deep
Or pathways lie so steep,
But we can go, if by God's power,
We only bear the burden by the hour.

life's clock

The clock of life is wound but once,
and no man has the power
To tell just where the hands will stop,
at late or early hour.

To lose one's wealth is sad indeed,
to lose one's health is more;
To lose one's soul is such a loss
as no man can restore.

The present is our own; live, love,
toil with a will;
Place no faith in tomorrow, for the
clock may then be still.

God bless you

God bless you and keep you
And give you His love.

God prosper your labor
With help from above.

Be His strength in your arm
And His love in your soul,

His smile your reward
And His glory your goal.

that you may "B" happy

B-patient, B prayerful, B humble, B mild,
B-wise as a solon, B meek as a child
B-studious, B thoughtful, B loving, B kind,
B-sure you make matter subservient to mind
B-cautious, B prudent, B trustful, B true,
B-courteous to all, B friendly with few,
B-temperate in argument, pleasure and wine,
B-careful of conduct, of money and time,
B-cheerful, B grateful, B hopeful, B firm,
B-peaceful, benevolent, willing to learn,
B-courageous, B gentle, B liberal and just,
B-aspiring, B humble because you are dust,
B-penitent, circumspect, sound in the faith,
B-active, devoted, B faithful 'til death,
B-honest, B holy, transparent and pure,
B-dependent, B Christ-like, and you'll be secure.

what is Christ to me?

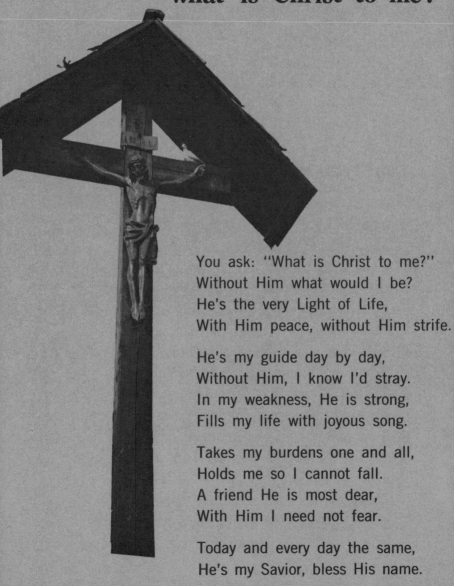

You ask: "What is Christ to me?"
Without Him what would I be?
He's the very Light of Life,
With Him peace, without Him strife.

He's my guide day by day,
Without Him, I know I'd stray.
In my weakness, He is strong,
Fills my life with joyous song.

Takes my burdens one and all,
Holds me so I cannot fall.
A friend He is most dear,
With Him I need not fear.

Today and every day the same,
He's my Savior, bless His name.

human relations

The most important 6 words:
"I admit I made a mistake."

The most important 5 words:
"I am proud of you."

The most important 4 words:
"What is your opinion?"

The most important 3 words:
"If you please."

The most important 2 words:
"Thank you."

The most important word:
"We."

And the least important word:
"I."

for those growing old

Lord, You know better than I know myself that I am growing older and will some day be old.

Keep me from the fatal habit of thinking I must say something on every subject and on every occasion.

Release me from craving to try to straighten out everybody's affairs.

Make me thoughtful, but not moody; helpful but not bossy.

With my vast store of wisdom, it seems a pity not to use it all, but You know, Lord, that I want a few friends.

Keep my mind free from the recital of endless details; give me wings to get to the point.

Seal my lips on my aches and pains. They are increasing, and the love of rehearsing them is becoming sweeter as the years go by.

I dare not ask for grace enough to enjoy the tales of others' pains, but help me to endure them with patience.

I dare not ask for improved memory, but for a growing humility and a lessening cocksureness when my memory seems to clash with the memories of others.

Teach me the glorious lesson that occasionally I may be mistaken.

Keep me reasonably sweet; I do not want to be a saint—some of them are so hard to live with—but a sour old person is one of the crowning works of the devil.

Give me the ability to see good things in unexpected places and talents in unexpected people.

And give me, Lord, the grace to tell them so.

Amen.

it shows in your face

You don't have to tell
            how you live each day;
You don't have to say
            if you work or play;

A tried, true barometer serves in the place,
However you live, it will show in your face.

The false, the deceit that you bear in your heart
Will not stay inside where it first got a start;

For sinew and blood are a thin veil of lace—
What you wear in your heart, you wear in your face.

If your life is unselfish, if for others you live,
For not what you get, but how much you
  can give;
If you live close to God in His infinite grace—
You don't have to tell it, it shows in your face.

when my temper flies

When I have lost my temper, I have
    lost my reason, too.
I'm never proud of anything which
    angrily I do.

When I have talked in anger and
    my cheeks are flaming
    red,
I have always uttered something
    which I wish I hadn't said.

In anger I have never done a
　　kindly deed or wise,
But many things for which I felt
　　I should apologize.

In looking back across my life and
　　all I've lost or made,
I can't recall a single time when
　　fury ever paid.

So I struggle to be patient, for I've
　　reached a wiser age;
I do not want to do a thing or
　　speak a word in rage.

I have learned by sad experience
　　that when my temper flies,
I never do a worthy thing,
　　a decent deed or wise.

When we believe ourselves to be alone
    He is there
    He hears us
    He loves us.

—St. Augustine

By myself, I can do nothing,
but with God,
I can do all things.

For the love of God
I want to do all things.

To Him,
the honor and the glory;
to me, the eternal reward.

—Fr. James Alberione, S.S.P.

"In the theology
of those who have faith,
chance is non-existent.
It is **God**
who watches over everything—
great and small. Solely in this way
is **peace** to be had."

— Fr. James Alberione, S.S.P.

Faith is the midnight
and God the coming day.

—St. John of the Cross

others

God, help me live from day to day
In such a self-forgetful way
That even when I kneel to pray,
My prayer shall be for —others.

Help me in all the work I do
To ever be sincere and true
And know that all I'd do for You,
I must do for —others.

And when my work on earth is done
And my new work in heaven's begun
May I forget the crown I've won
While thinking still of —others.

Others, God, yes, others,
Let this my motto be.
Help me to live for others,
That I might live like Thee.

teach me

Lord   Teach me to be generous;
Teach me to serve You
as You deserve:

To give without counting the cost,
To fight without heeding the wounds,
To toil without looking for rest,
To work without asking for a reward
Except the reward of knowing
that I am doing Your will.

—St. Ignatius Loyola

sowing

Sow a thought and you will
         reap an act;
Sow an act and you will
         reap a habit;
Sow a habit and you will
         reap a character;
Sow a character and you will
         reap a destiny!

—Fr. James Alberione, S.S.P.

if

If there is righteousness in the heart,
there will be beauty in the character;

If there be beauty in the character,
there will be harmony in the home;

If there be harmony in the home,
there will be order in the nation;

When there is order in the nation,
there will be peace in the world.

working girl's prayer

Dear Lord,
    I just don't have the time
    To say an aspiration;
    My typing, shorthand, and the rest
    Crowd out all meditation.

    I'd like to say a prayer or two
    While working through the day,
    But "Yours received" and "We regret"
    Are always in the way.

    I know that You will understand
    And bless a girl who tries
    So if it's all the same to You,
    Dear Lord, we'll compromise.

    Each time I type a manuscript,
    I'm praying on the keys,
    The M's are all "Hail Mary's,"
    The G's are "Glory Be's."

    And when I take a memo, Lord,
    I'll pray to you again,
    Each word will mean "Laudate!"
    Each period, "Amen."

49

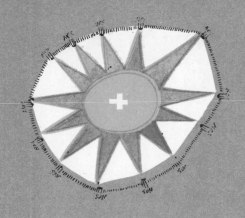

the teen commandments

1. Don't let your parents down—they brought you up.
2. Be humble enough to obey—you'll be giving orders yourself some day.
3. Stop and think before you drink.
4. At the first moment turn away from unclean thinking.
5. Don't show off when driving—if you want to race, go to Indianapolis.
6. Choose a date who would make a good mate.
7. Go to church faithfully. The Creator gives you a week—give Him back one hour.
8. Avoid following the crowd—be an engine not a caboose.
9. Choose your companions carefully—you will become what they are.
10. Keep the Ten Commandments.

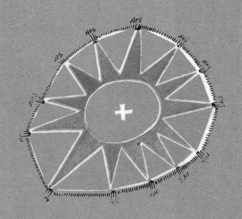

still in vogue...

I, the Lord, am your God:

    I. You shall not have strange gods before me.

    II. You shall not take the name of the Lord your God in vain.

    III. Remember to keep holy the Lord's day.

    IV. Honor your father and your mother.

    V. You shall not kill.

    VI. You shall not commit adultery.

    VII. You shall not steal.

    VIII. You shall not bear false witness against your neighbor.

    IX. You shall not covet your neighbor's wife.

    X. You shall not covet your neighbor's goods.

for those
who live alone

I live alone, dear Lord,
Stay by my side,
In all my daily needs
Be Thou my guide.

52

Grant me good health,
For that indeed, I pray,
To carry on my work
from day to day.

Keep pure my mind,
My thoughts, my every deed,
Let me be kind, unselfish
In my neighbor's need.

Spare me from fire, from flood,
Malicious tongues,
From thieves, from fear,
And evil ones.

If sickness or an accident befall,
Then humbly, Lord, I pray,
Hear Thou my call.

And when I'm feeling low,
Or in despair,
Lift up my heart
And help me in my prayer.

I live alone, dear Lord,
Yet have no fear,
Because I feel Your presence
Ever near. Amen.

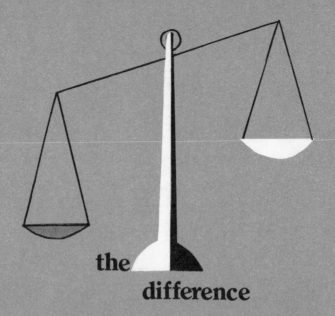

the difference

I got up early one morning
And rushed right into the
    day;
I had so much to accomplish
That I didn't take time to pray.

Problems just tumbled
    about me,
And heavier came each task;
"Why doesn't God help me?"
    I wondered,
He answered: "You didn't
    ask."

I wanted to see joy and beauty
But the day toiled on, gray
    and bleak;
I wondered why God didn't
    show me,
He said: "But you didn't seek."

I tried to come into God's
    presence,
I used all my keys at the
    lock.
God gently and lovingly
    chided,
"My child, you didn't knock."

I woke up early this morning,
And paused before entering the day;
I had so much to accomplish
That I had to take time to pray.

when you are tired, discouraged and blue

Just close your eyes
and open your heart
And feel your worries
and cares depart,

Just yield yourself
to the Father above

And let Him hold you
secure in His love—

For life on earth
grows more involved

With endless problems
that can't be solved—

But God only asks us
to do our best,

Then He will "take over"
and finish the rest.

So when you are tired,
discouraged and blue,

There's only one door
that is open to you—

And that is the door
to "The House of Prayer"

And you'll find God waiting
to meet you there.

"3"

Three things to be—
    pure, just and honest.
Three things to govern—
    temper, tongue and conduct.
Three things to have—
    courage, affection and gentleness.
Three things to give—
    alms to the needy, comfort to the sad and
    appreciation to the worthy.
Three things to love—
    the wise, the virtuous and the innocent.
Three things to commend—
    thrift, industry and promptness.
Three things to despise—
    cruelty, arrogance and ingratitude.
Three things to attain—
    goodness of heart, integrity of purpose
    and cheerfulness.

there's a reason

For ev'ry pain, that we must bear,
For ev'ry burden, ev'ry care,

                  There's a reason.

For ev'ry grief, that bows the head,
For ev'ry tear-drop that is shed,

                  There's a reason.

For ev'ry hurt, for ev'ry plight,
For ev'ry lonely, pain-racked night,

                  There's a reason.

But if we trust God, as we should,
It all will work out for our good,

                  He knows the reason.

my path

God wills that I reach heaven
and He grants me the means.

All I have to do is give my consent:

to decide to walk

the path

the Lord

has marked

out for me

and walk it well.

Fr. James Alberione, S.S.P.

I know something good about you

Wouldn't this old world be better
If the folks we meet would say,
"I know something good about you!"
And then treat us just that way?

Wouldn't it be fine and dandy
If each handclasp warm and true
Carried with it this assurance,
"I know something good about you!"

Wouldn't life be lots more happy,
If the good that's in us all
Were the only thing about us
That folks bothered to recall?

Wouldn't life be lots more happy,
If we praised the good we see?—
For there's such a lot of goodness
In the worst of you and me.

Wouldn't it be nice to practice
That fine way of thinking, too?—
You know something good about me!
I know something good about you!

in praise of virtue

Where there is charity and wisdom,
there is neither fear nor ignorance.

Where there is patience and humility,
there is neither anger nor loss of composure.

Where there is poverty borne with joy,
there is neither grasping nor hoarding.

Where there is quiet and meditation,
there is neither worry nor dissipation.

Where there is the fear of the Lord to guard the
    gateway,
there the enemy can get no hold for an entry.

Where there is mercy and discernment,
there is neither luxury nor a hardened heart.

—St. Francis of Assisi

our people

I've just been thinking all day long,
And I just can't see
Why I talk about you
And you talk about me.

The biggest drawback to our people
And I know that you agree
Are the things I say about you
And the things you say about me.

If you see a person digging
For a higher hope or stakes
Don't try to make it hard for him
By whispering around his mistakes.

You make mistakes you know;
I make them too, I find.
I don't intend to broadcast yours
So please don't broadcast mine.

I think a lot about our people,
I wish that it could be,
An example for every person
In this land of liberty.

So let this be our slogan,
Our world would grander be,
If I don't talk about you —
And you don't talk about me.

advice

If your troubles are
Deep-seated and long-standing,
Try kneeling.

When'er you pass a church,
Always make a visit,
So that when you're carried there
Our Lord won't ask, "Who is it?"

judge not

Pray do not find fault with the man
who limps or stumbles along the road
unless you have worn the shoes he wears
or struggled beneath his load.

Don't sneer at the man who's down today
unless you have felt the blow
that caused his fall or felt the shame
that only the fallen know.

Don't be harsh with the man who sins
or pelt him with word or stone
unless you are sure, yes, doubly sure,
that you have no sins of your own.

believing

This is
    not a time
for believing
    everyone.

Believe only those
whom you see
modeling their lives
on the life of Christ.

—St. Teresa of Avila
"Way of Perfection"

stairs of
opportunity

The stairs of opportunity
Are sometimes hard to climb;
And that can only well be done
By one step at a time.

But he who would go to the top
Ne'er sits down and despairs;
Instead of staring up those steps
He just steps up the stairs!

how to count

Count your blessings
  instead of your crosses,
Count your gains
  instead of your losses,
Count your joys
  instead of your woes,
Count your friends
  instead of your foes,
Count your smiles
  instead of your tears,
Count your courage
  instead of your fears,
Count your full years
  instead of your lean,
Count your kind deeds
  instead of your mean,
Count your health
  instead of your wealth,
Count on God
  instead of yourself.

I'll go where You want me to go

I'll go where You want me to go, dear Lord.
Over mountain or plain or sea
I'll do what You want me to do, dear Lord.
I'll be what You want me to be.
It may not be on the mountain top, or over
   the stormy sea
It may not be at the battle front,
The Lord will have need of me.

But if by a still, small voice He calls,
To lands that I do not know,
I'll answer, dear Lord, with my hand in Yours,
I'll go where You want me to go.

There's surely a lowly place somewhere,
In earth's harvest field—so wide
Where I may labor through life's short day,
For Jesus the crucified.

So trusting my all to Your tender care,
And knowing Your love for me,

I'll do
Your will
with heart sincere,
I'll be what You want me to be.

your cross

The everlasting God has in His wisdom foreseen from eternity the cross that He now presents to you as a gift from His inmost heart.

This cross He now sends you He has considered with His all-knowing eyes, understood with His divine mind, tested with His wise justice, warmed with loving arms, and weighed with His own hands to see that it be not one inch too large and not one ounce too heavy for you.

He has blessed it with His holy name, anointed it with His grace, perfumed it with His consolation, taken one last glance at you and your courage, and then sent it to you from heaven—a special greeting from God to you, an alms of the all-merciful love of God.

—St. Francis de Sales

be at peace

Do not look forward to what might happen
 tomorrow.
The same everlasting Father
who cares for you today
will take care of you
tomorrow and every day....
Either He will shield you from suffering, or
He will give you unfailing strength to bear it.
Be at peace then and put aside all anxious
thoughts and imaginations.

—St. Francis de Sales

even if ...

Even
if you
cannot
always
be joyful,
you can
always
be at
peace.

—Mother Thecla Merlo

mother's heart

Sacred chalice—
 the heart of a mother,
 possessing God above.

 Should waters cease to flow,
 should nations part,

And yet still beat
 a mother's heart,

That alone
 would be the proof

Of God's unchanging love.

power of prayer

Prayer is man's strength
and God's weakness.

—St. Augustine

Christ of Calvary

O Christ of Calvary—there to die for sins of mine
And full redemption of human kind
Shall I so live—and die—to no avail
And find myself without the pale of Thy redemptive
    love?
Does not the shedding of Thy blood
On Calvary's leafless tree
Tell the story of Thy love for me?

What loving story can I tell to Thee?
My sins I see in flaming welts across Thy back.
O God, is there no help for me?
My sins are in the thorns that pierce Thy head.
Is Thy saving cross a total loss for me?
My sins are in the nails that bind with bloody
    thongs Thy flesh to wood.
My sins are in the spear that opened wide
    Thy side.

O Christ, is there no hope? Answer me!
And from the cross came Christ's reply, "Son,
    behold Thy mother."
O Mother of Christ, in His last dying word to me
I hear the secret of eternity—
To Christ through thee.
No Judas rope for me!
And I replied, "Mother, behold thy son."

—Fr. James P. Donohue

beatitudes

for friends of the aged

Blessed are they who understand
My faltering step and palsied hand.

Blessed are they who know that my ears today
Must strain to catch the things they say.

Blessed are they who seem to know
That my eyes are dim and my wits are slow.

Blessed are they who looked away
When coffee spilled at table today.

Blessed are they with a cheery smile
Who stop to chat for a little while.

Blessed are they who never say,
"You've told that story twice today."

Blessed are they who know the ways
To bring back memories of yesterdays.

Blessed are they who make it known
That I'm loved, respected and not alone.

Blessed are they who know I'm at a loss
To find the strength to carry the cross.

Blessed are they who ease the days
On my journey Home in loving ways.

—Esther Mary Walker

chosen one

When God gave me a cross to bear
I had no feeling of utter despair
But wondered what I had ever done
That I should be His chosen one.

I did not ask the reason why
Our blessed Lord would think that I
Possessed the virtue of resignation
Or had the merit of mortification.

He, who knows all, has sought me out,
Whatever He asks, I'll never doubt,
It's an honor great to do His task
And never will I a question ask.

Though answers have been a million fold
In my heart the secret I hold.
Aren't I lucky to think that He
With all the world—selected me!

take time...

Take time to think
      it is the source of power

Take time to play
      it is the secret of youth

Take time to read
      it is the fount of wisdom

Take time to be friendly
      it is the road to happiness

Take time to laugh
      it is the music of the soul

Take time to meditate and pray
      it is the lifting up of mind and heart to God.

IFE

is a blend of the good and the bad,
    A bit of the glad and a bit of the sad;
    A pinch of contentment, a time of unrest,
    A dash of the worst and a lot of the best;
    A little of failure, a little of luck,
    A bit of disaster and plenty of pluck;

And who would live long
must be willing to know
    That God is our Master
    wherever we go.

Daughters of St. Paul

IN MASSACHUSETTS
> 50 St. Paul's Avenue, Boston, Ma. 02130
> 172 Tremont Street, Boston, Ma. 02111

IN NEW YORK
> 78 Fort Place, Staten Island, N.Y. 10301
> 59 East 43rd St., New York, N.Y. 10017
> 625 East 187th Street, Bronx, N.Y. 10458
> 525 Main Street, Buffalo, N.Y. 14203

IN NEW JERSEY
> 84 Washington Street, Bloomfield, N.J. 07003

IN CONNECTICUT
> 202 Fairfield Avenue, Bridgeport, Ct. 06604

IN OHIO
> 2105 Ontario St. (at Prospect Ave.), Cleveland, Oh. 44115
> 25 E. Eighth Street, Cincinnati, Oh. 45202

IN PENNSYLVANIA
> 1719 Chestnut St., Philadelphia, Pa. 19103

IN FLORIDA
> 2700 Biscayne Blvd., Miami, Fl. 33137

IN LOUISIANA
> 4403 Veterans Memorial Blvd., Metairie, La. 70002
> 1800 South Acadian Thruway, P.O. Box 2028, Baton Rouge, La. 70802

IN MISSOURI
> 1001 Pine St. (at North 10th), St. Louis, Mo. 63101

IN TEXAS
> 114 East Main Plaza, San Antonio, Tx. 78205

IN CALIFORNIA
> 1570 Fifth Avenue, San Diego, Ca. 92101
> 46 Geary Street, San Francisco, Ca. 94108

IN HAWAII
> 1184 Bishop St., Honolulu, Hi. 96813

IN ALASKA
> 750 West 5th Avenue, Anchorage, Ak. 99501

IN CANADA
> 3022 Dufferin Street, Toronto 395, Ontario, Canada

IN ENGLAND
> 57, Kensington Church Street, London W. 8, England

IN AUSTRALIA
> 58, Abbotsford Rd., Homebush, N.S.W., Sydney 2140, Australia

Smile!
God loves you